The Beginner's Guide to Macramé

First published in 2026
Search Press Limited
Wellwood, North Farm Road,
Tunbridge Wells, Kent TN2 3DR

1 2 3 4 5 6 7 8 9 10

ISBN: 978-1-80092-365-2
ebook ISBN: 978-1-80093-349-1

Editor: Carrie Baker
Managing Editor: Becky Robbins
Head of Design: Marrianne Miall
Publishing Director: Samantha Warrington

Bookmarked Hub

For further ideas and inspiration, and to join our free online community, visit www.bookmarkedhub.com

Publishers' notes

Metric measurements are used in this book; the imperial conversions are rounded to the nearest ¼in. Always use either metric or imperial measurements, not a combination of both.

For errata, please visit our website (www.searchpress.com) or the Bookmarked Hub (www.bookmarkedhub.com).

GPSR information can be found at www.searchpress.com
Printed in China, TT112025

Dedication

This book is dedicated to all the creative and brave souls who have chosen to learn the ancient art of macramé with a beginner's mind. Happy knotting!

Acknowledgements

I would like to thank Search Press for helping me bring this book to life and for sharing my passion with all the curious souls ready to learn macramé.

To all the wonderful people I've had the pleasure of teaching over the years, thank you. I've learned just as much from you as you may have from me, and your questions, feedback and enthusiasm helped shape this book into something clear, approachable and beginner friendly.

A heartfelt thank you to my family, who continue to inspire, support and uplift me throughout my creative journey. To my husband and my girls – thank you for your patience, love and honest feedback.

And finally, to my amazing macramé community – thank you for following, encouraging and supporting my work. Your kindness and connection mean the world.

ISABELLA STRAMBIO

The Beginner's Guide to Macramé

Easy techniques and 8 fun projects

SEARCH PRESS

Contents

Introduction

Macramé, the art of knotting, is one of the oldest crafts known to humanity. I love how simple knots can be transformed into intricate patterns, creating both beautiful and functional everyday items. My own journey with macramé began by chance, but the moment I tied my first knot, I was hooked. There was something mesmerizing about the rhythm of knotting – the mindfulness it encouraged and the endless creative possibilities it offered. I could immediately see the potential of this craft, and I knew it would become a lifelong passion.

Since then, macramé has been a constant source of inspiration for me. I've been teaching macramé since 2016, and I've witnessed firsthand the positive impact it has on people. It's an incredible way to express creativity, develop personal style and experience the joy of making something with your own hands.

One of the things I love most about macramé is its versatility. Whether you're working with fine cords to create delicate jewellery or using thick ropes to craft bold wall hangings and furniture, the possibilities are endless. You can make intricate decorations or practical items like bags, clothing and home accessories – all tailored to your personal taste and style.

Another reason macramé is so popular is the time commitment (or lack thereof). As a beginner, you can complete a simple project, like the keychain on page 40, in under an hour. Unlike some crafts that require days or weeks of effort, macramé offers quick rewards, making it accessible to everyone. The sense of accomplishment that comes from finishing a piece boosts confidence and motivation, keeping you excited to create more.

Beyond creativity, macramé also has incredible mental health benefits. Working with your hands, feeling the texture of natural materials and following the rhythmic movements of knotting can be deeply therapeutic. It helps reduce stress, anxiety and even feelings of loneliness. The repetitive motions encourage a flow state, where your mind becomes fully engaged in the task, promoting relaxation and a sense of calm. Plus, completing a project releases dopamine – a feel-good chemical – lifting your mood and enhancing your overall well-being.

Macramé isn't just a craft; it's a way to express yourself, unwind and connect with a vibrant community of makers. So, welcome to the world of macramé! I hope this book inspires you to embrace the journey with a beginner's mind.

Happy knotting!
Isabella

How to use this book

Starting a new craft is exciting, but it can also feel a little daunting – especially if you haven't done anything creative in a while. That's where this book comes in! It's designed to be your perfect guide as you begin your macramé journey.

The first section introduces you to the materials and basic tools you'll need. Before diving into the projects, I recommend practising a few knots with some spare string to build your confidence and work on your the tension of your knots (see page 24 for more on tension). Once you're comfortable with the basics, you'll be ready to start your first project!

Begin with simpler designs that use just one or two knots, like the Keychain on page 40 or Hat Décor on page 58. As you progress through the book, the projects gradually increase in complexity, helping you develop new techniques and refine your skills. By the time you reach the larger projects, such as the Owl or the Wall Hanging (pages 76 and 108), you'll be combining multiple knots and crafting more intricate designs.

Each project includes step-by-step tutorials to introduce new knots and techniques, ensuring that, by the end of this book, you'll feel confident in your macramé skills and ready to create more beautiful macramé pieces.

Working safely

When working on macramé, cotton dust can accumulate from the strings. If you suffer from asthma or have children or pets in your home, it's important to vacuum your workspace after each session to keep the air clean.

Be sure to store loose strings on a high shelf or in a cupboard when you're not working on your piece, especially if you have young children or pets around. This helps to prevent any risk of suffocation or accidental tripping.

Macramé can also be physically demanding if done for long periods. Your hands, shoulders and back may start to ache, so it's essential to maintain good posture. Avoid hunching over your work, take regular breaks and stretch your hands and shoulders. A short pause for a cup of tea or a few minutes of movement can help keep your body comfortable and reduce strain.

Tools and materials

The great thing about macramé is that you don't need many tools, especially to begin with, and you can make most of the projects in this book on a flat surface like your kitchen or dining table. Here is the essential toolkit to get started.

BASIC TOOLS

1. MEASURING TAPE

Use to measure your strings accurately.

2. SHARP SCISSORS

You will need small, sharp scissors to cut the strings and also to trim the final fringes of your macramé.

3. CORK/MACRAMÉ BOARD

If you choose to work on a macramé board, fix your strings using pins. This makes your work portable, which also gives you the flexibility to work at a table or on your lap. Macramé boards can be purchased online. Alternatively you can use a plain cork mat or pin board.

4. PINS

Use dressmaking pins with a large head to secure your work to your macramé board.

5. COMB OR PET BRUSH

You can use a basic plastic comb or a pet brush to brush the fringe at the end of some of the projects. See page 25 for more on brushing fringes.

6. BEADER OR CROCHET HOOK (OPTIONAL)

A beader is a long tool often used to help thread beads onto string. It can also be used to tuck in string ends on the reverse of your macramé projects. Alternatively, you can use a crochet hook, as shown opposite.

7. SEWING NEEDLE

A large-eyed tapestry needle (not pictured) is useful for securing loose string ends or adding more string if you run out mid-project (see more on page 38).

6
5.0mm
5
3
1
2
4
60 in

MATERIALS

1. STRING

Cotton string is the most common type of string used in macramé. It is readily available at craft stores and online. Strings come in various types – such as single twist, 3-ply and braided – and different thicknesses, usually measured in millimetres. Cotton cord is popular for its softness, knotting ease and natural look. See more on choosing string for your projects overleaf.

2. DOWELS & WOODEN STICKS

Dowels and sticks are used in some of the projects either to hang your work from, such as the Wall Hanging (page 108) or for added decorative effects such as the Owl project (page 76). You can buy wooden dowels from your local craft store or DIY shop. Alternatively, you could collect driftwood or fallen branches from your local surroundings. In the latter case, use an old brush to clean your wooden stick with water and let it dry outside in the sun before using it, making sure there are no insects on it.

3. FABRIC GLUE OR GLUE GUN

Add a dab of glue to secure finished string ends.

4. MASKING TAPE

Use masking tape to fix your strings onto a flat surface and to tape the end of your strings to prevent fraying or to help you thread beads.

5. BEADS

Beads can be added to any piece for extra interest. I have used large wooden beads for eyes in the Owl project.

6. METAL FRAMES

Metal frames hold the shape of your work and you can knot directly onto the frame. They are readily available in different sizes and finishes from craft stores and online. I have used a round frame for the Owl, and a lampshade frame for the project (page 90).

7. CLASPS

A swivel lobster clasp is used for the Keychain project (page 40), readily available in different sizes from craft stores or online.

8. S HOOKS (OPTIONAL)

You can use these hooks to hang your macramé projects while you work. Try hanging them on a rail, the back of a chair, door or architrave.

9. CLOTHES RAIL (OPTIONAL)

You might find it useful to hang your macramé projects on a clothes rail (not pictured) while you work. Any rail is fine but, ideally, you want one on castors and adjustable in height.

6
4
2
3
PVA Glue
80ml
5
7
8

STRING

With macramé, you can use any type of string. However, the beauty of modern macramé, compared with the more traditional macramé that was popular in the 1970s, is the availability of cotton string in a variety of colours, which is much more enjoyable to work with than jute and twine. In this book, I used recycled cotton string in two different variations:

Braided string Perfect for beginners! Soft and sturdy, this type of string has a modern look and feel, and it doesn't unravel. It's slightly stretchy, so don't pull it when you measure and cut your strings, or you will end up with shorter strings than needed, which might affect your project.

Single-twist string This is the softest string. It's beautiful to touch and work with, but it's more delicate; it can unravel quickly, and it is less forgiving if you don't keep consistent tension. Because it unravels easily, it's the perfect choice for macramé with brushed fringes. The final look is soft, smooth and lush.

Both these types of string come in a range of colours and sizes from 1.5mm to 9mm.

Remember that all the projects can be easily adapted to your taste and style, including choosing your preferred colours and thickness of string.

As a beginner, I would recommend you start by choosing your favourite colour for your projects and later, if you feel adventurous, try experimenting with different types of strings and thickness.

Below, left to right: Braided string, single twist, 3-ply, bamboo braided, bamboo single twist, felt string.

OTHER COMMON TYPES OF STRING

3-ply string This is another popular type of cotton string used in macramé. It's made from three individual strands twisted together to make one rope.

Bamboo string This type of string comes in braided or single twist. It has a slight sheen to it, and it feels very soft. However, it's the most delicate type of string, and it unravels very easily and quickly. I would recommend this type of string to more confident macramé makers.

Felt string Made from wool, this is a great alternative for a natural look and feel.

CUTTING STRING

Accurately measuring and cutting your string is essential to ensure you don't run out before completing your macramé project. If you do run out of string, see pages 38–39 for how to add more mid-project. Always use a measuring tape and cut each piece individually to maintain precision. While slight variations in length are normal, try to keep differences within a few centimetres (or up to an inch).

If you're using braided string, be aware that it has some stretch. Avoid pulling the string while measuring, as this can lead to incorrect lengths. Instead, gently place the string alongside your measuring tape and cut carefully.

Tips

It is important to buy enough string for your whole project at the same time, to ensure that it's from the same dye lot. Look for the dye lot on the string's label. The dyeing process can result in the string from a different dye batch being a very slightly different colour, as well a slightly different thickness. Using different dye lots or thicknesses in the same project could be noticeable and spoil your finished project.

Keep any scraps of string that are longer than 50cm (around 20in) as they can be used for future projects like adding colourful fringes to a wall hanging.

READING A STRING LABEL

Not all string labels are the same, but you will usually find the essentials for your project printed on the string label: the thickness of the string, the material it is made of, its meterage and its colour name.

1 The type of string
2 Thickness of the string
3 Name of manufacturer
4 Length, in metres
5 The colour name (and sometimes the dye lot)
6 Yarn composition
7 Laundry and care instructions
8 Country of origin

Macramé essentials

Starting your macramé journey can be both exciting and a little overwhelming. Here are some must-know techniques that will help you work through your macramé projects with confidence.

MACRAMÉ TERMINOLOGY

Just like any craft, macramé has its own set of essential terms that are helpful to learn before starting a project. Knowing these basics will make it easier to follow patterns, understand tutorials and enjoy the creative process.

Macramé terminology is simple, and you don't need to memorize a long list to get started!

Filler strings or **Anchor strings**	The stationary strings on which knots are tied, providing the structure to the design.
Fringe	The loose ends of strings that hang down from a macramé piece, which can be trimmed for a decorative effect.
Sinnet or **Sennit**	A series of consecutive identical knots.
String or **Cord**	The primary material used in macramé. Strings come in various types (see page 16).
Working string	The strings used to tie knots and patterns.

Tip

In the project instructions, the working strings are often referred to by numbers, for example strings 1–4. Count the strings from left to right (see an example on page 35).

HOW TO COUNT KNOTS

When following or creating macramé patterns, it is useful to understand how to count in rows.

Rows The horizontal lines of knots, moving from top to bottom as you build your design. In the first example below, you can see 19 rows of alternating square knots.

Line of knots Each row is made of a full line of knots. In the image opposite, you can see a row of 16 square knots in a line.

Once you get the hang of it, counting becomes second nature and makes reading patterns much easier.

COUNTING ROWS

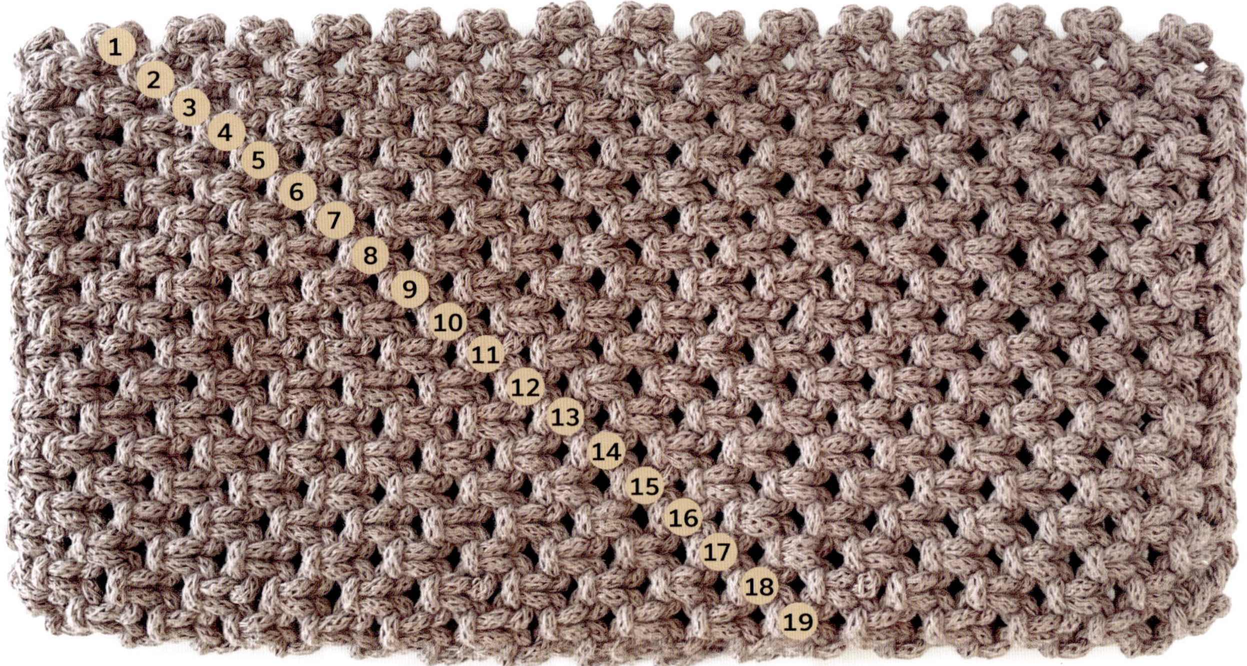

COUNTING KNOTS IN A LINE

Tip

If you are making a macramé piece with many rows of the same knot, such as in the macramé Clutch Bag (see page 64), you can use a crochet or knitting stitch counter to keep track of the rows you are knotting.

TENSION

Just like with other crafts such as knitting or crochet, tension in macramé varies from person to person. Some knotters work tightly, while others naturally have looser work. The key is to maintain consistency throughout your project. As long as your knots are uniform and clearly defined, slight variations in tightness won't affect the final result. However, be mindful not to make your knots too loose, as this can cause your design to lose structure.

You can see from the examples above how tension that is too tight or too loose can alter your finished knots.

1 Tight knot tension: your project will turn out smaller than planned.

2 Average knot tension: your project should turn out neatly and as planned.

3 Looser knot tension: your projects may be slightly larger than planned.

4 Very loose knot tension: this is less ideal and may not result in a neat, good-quality final project.

BRUSHING A FRINGE

Brushing a fringe is very satisfying and will complete your macramé piece with a neat look. For the best result use a comb or pet brush.

1 Cut the strings at the approximate desired length (note that after unravelling, the length of the strings will increase slightly).

2 If you are using 3-ply string, start from the top of each string, unravel the three strands by twisting the string and running your fingers through it. Each strand is made up of finer strings – unravel those too.

3 Once you have unravelled all the strings, use a comb or pet brush to tidy the fringe. It will look fuller and smoother. Make sure you don't brush too hard, or you might break the finer strings.

4 You may want to trim your fringe again after brushing.

BRUSHING A SINGLE TWIST FRINGE

If you are using a single-twist string, you can skip to step 3, as shown above, before continuing with the steps below.

1 Start brushing the bottom of the strings and work your way upwards.

2 Trim your piece again to finish.

TRIMMING A FRINGE

A neatly trimmed fringe will give your macramé projects a sleek and professional finish. You can trim freehand, or you might like to use a template as a straight edge to help achieve a neat, straight line.

1 Cut a cardboard template with straight edges.

2 Brush the fringe as explained on page 25. Trim the fringe with sharp scissors, using the template as your guide.

Tip

Another way you can trim the fringe is to use masking tape to mark the end of the fringe, then cut the strings below the tape.

You will brush and trim the fringe shown here in the Owl project (see page 76).

Tips for success

As you are starting your macramé journey, a few simple tips can make your macramé learning experience smoother, more enjoyable and even more creative. Here is my practical advice to help you avoid common mistakes, stay organized and get the best results from your projects.

WORKING WITH LONG STRINGS

When you make a large-scale macramé piece you will have very long strings. My advice is to bundle each string to make the process of tying knots easier and quicker and avoid any tangling. It is also a safety measure to prevent you tripping over the strings. Simply fold the strings several times and tie a knot around them, or use a rubber band. This process can be time-consuming, but it's worth it.

On larger projects, tie long strings together to avoid tangles or unwanted knots.

PREVENTING YOUR STRINGS UNRAVELLING

When you use single-twist strings, the ends will unravel very quickly. Tape the ends with masking tape as soon as you have cut each piece. This step can be time-consuming, but it is necessary if you want to avoid the strings getting tangled or damaged.

Add masking tape to string ends to stop them unravelling while you work.

IF YOU MAKE A MISTAKE

If you make a mistake with your macramé piece, you can simply undo the knots and redo them again, or accept the mistake as part of the piece. The best tip I can give you is to keep checking your piece for mistakes, especially if you are making a large item.

HIDING STRING ENDS

You will want to hide the string ends neatly when you finish your projects.

1 Tape the end with a piece of masking tape. Pass it through the back of one or two knots.

2 Trim the excess string.

3 Add a dot of fabric glue to secure the end (optional).

MAKING A KNOT WITH MULTIPLE STRINGS

Using multiple strings to make a square knot can change the look of the knot and your macramé piece.

On the right is a square knot worked with double strings. To do this, follow the same steps for the square knot (see page 44), but increase the number of strings for your working strings and the fillers. When pulling the knots, make sure the strings don't overlap but sit next to each other and lie flat. You will use this technique in the Clutch Bag project (page 64).

Looking after your macramé pieces

After all the time and care you've put into your projects, you need to store or display them carefully to keep them looking beautiful!

CARING FOR YOUR MACRAMÉ PIECES

Dust regularly Dust accumulation can dull the appearance of macramé. You can take your macramé outside and give it a gentle shake to dislodge any dirt or use a soft brush or lint roller (my preferred option) to gently remove dust from your macramé pieces.

Avoid direct sunlight Prolonged exposure to sunlight can cause fading and weakening of macramé fibres. Display your creations away from direct sunlight when possible to minimize damage, or rotate the location of your macramé piece.

Spot clean Use a damp cloth or sponge. Be very gentle and avoid excessive rubbing. You can use lukewarm water or a natural cleanser such as vinegar, if required.

Store properly When not in use, store your macramé creations in a clean, dry place away from moisture and humidity.

Tip

When hanging or displaying fringed macramé items, the fringes will need to be brushed regularly to keep the piece looking neat and tidy.

Techniques

and projects

Techniques

REVERSED LARK'S HEAD KNOT

The reversed lark's head knot is a simple yet useful variation of the basic lark's head knot, which you will learn on page 45.

1 Start with one string folded in half to create a loop in the centre of the string. Place your dowel over the loop.

2 Fold the loop of string over to the front of the support, then pull the two long strands through the loop.

3 Pull tight.

HALF SQUARE KNOT

This knot is mostly used with other half square knots to create a twisted effect.

1 Start with two lark's head knots (see page 45). Bring working string 1 over the filler strings (2 and 3) heading right. Pass it under working string 4.

2 Move working string 4 to the left, passing it under the filler strings and over working string 1. Pull on both working strings to tighten the knot, while holding the middle strings steady.

3 Pull tight.

GATHERING KNOT

This knot is usually used to start and finish a macramé piece. It's shown here in a contrasting colour string for clarity.

1 Fold a piece of string, shown here in cream.

2 Take the long, working end and wrap it around all the strings several times, as shown. You can wrap clockwise or anticlockwise: it will have the same outcome.

3 Keep wrapping the string around, arranging it below the previous wraps; continue until you are close to the folded loop. Pass the end of the string through the loop.

4 Pull the top string until it traps the bottom string underneath the knot. Cut both string ends.

You will make a gathering knot to give a neat finish to the Keychain project (see page 40).

ADDING MORE STRING MID-PROJECT

Running out of string halfway through a project happens to everyone! There are a few ways you can add additional strings to finish your piece. Before you add the new string, make sure you leave a long tail at the end of the old string. Once your piece is complete, you will need to weave the tails at the back of your macramé using a large-eyed tapestry needle to secure them, then snip the ends (see page 29).

ADDING A STRING WITH A SQUARE KNOT

1 Place the two working strings up behind the dowel and out of the way. These are the strings you are replacing.

2 Place the new folded string behind the two filler strings.

3 Make a square knot using the new working strings and existing filler strings (see page 44).

4 Tie the knot firmly. Once your piece is complete, use a large-eyed tapestry needle to weave the tails in at the back of your macramé, then cut the ends.

ADDING A STRING WITH A DOUBLE HALF HITCH KNOT

1 Take the short string (the one that needs replacing) to the back of the macramé and place the new string behind the filler string (this string is sometimes called the 'holding' or 'static' cord).

2 Tie a double half hitch knot (see page 62) using the new string.

3 Place the top end of the new string behind the macramé.

4 Tie the other strings using the double half hitch. Once your piece is complete, use a large-eyed tapestry needle to weave the tails at the back of your macramé, then cut the ends.

Keychain

This macramé keychain is the perfect beginner project – small, quick and incredibly satisfying to make. This project is great to practise some of the basic macramé knots, use up leftover cord and create something both stylish and practical. Whether clipped to your keys or bag, or gifted to a friend, this project is a fun way to dip your toes into the world of macramé.

SIZE

18cm (7in) long, including clasp

MATERIALS

- 2.5m (2½yd) of 3mm braided string
- 1 x swivel lobster claw clasp

TOOLS

- Measuring tape
- Scissors

KNOTS USED

- Gathering knot (page 36)
- Half square knot (page 35)
- Reversed lark's head knot (page 34)

CUT

- 2 x 2m (2yd) of string
- 1 x 50cm (19½in) of string

Instructions

1 Tie two strings, each measuring 2m (2yd) long, onto the lobster clasp with reversed lark's head knot. Ensure the middle two strands are each 50cm (19½in) long, so the outer two strands will each be around 1.5m (1¾yd) long.

2 Leave a gap of 3cm (1¼in) and tie a sinnet of half square knots, until you almost run out of string or reach 20–30cm (7–12in) in length.

3 Fold the macramé to make sure you are happy with the finished size.

4 Use the 50cm (19½in) length of string to tie a gathering knot around the ends, covering the gap at the top.

5 Trim any excess strings to finish.

Techniques

SQUARE KNOT

This is the most important and most-often used knot in macramé, as well as the most versatile. I always tie left-facing square knots for consistency, but you can make them right-facing if you want, as long as you are consistent within each project.

1 Make a left-facing half square knot (see page 35).

2 Move working string 4 to the left, passing it over the fillers and under working string 1. Move working string 1 to the right, passing under the fillers and over string 4.

3 Tighten the square knot by pulling on the working strings, while holding the middle strings steady and making sure they are not overlapping.

Tip

Tying left- or right-facing square knots is a matter of preference. The majority of macramé pieces will be knotted with the left-facing square knot. My advice is to try both and see which one you prefer.

LARK'S HEAD KNOT

This knot is used to attach a folded string to the support – a piece of driftwood, a dowel, ring or another string.

1 Fold the string in half and place it on top of the support where the knot will be tied.

2 Fold the loop of string behind the support, without twisting the strings, then pull the two long strands through the loop.

3 Pull tight.

ALTERNATING SQUARE KNOT

This is the most common and simple pattern in macramé. By changing the gap between the rows of square knots you can create different looks and net-like effects.

1 Tie a row of square knots (see page 44).

Tip

Alternating square knots is a pattern you will be using regularly. If you add a gap in between the rows you will create a net-look, like in the Bottle Holder project on page 48.

2 Start the second row by making a square knot using strings 3 and 4 from the first square knot and strings 1 and 2 from the second square knot. Continue making square knots with the remaining strings, leaving the last two strings untouched. You will have two unused strings on both the left and the right.

3 Repeat steps 1 and 2 until you reach the desired length. When you start row 3, make sure you keep your first square knot horizontal – you will have a gap between your new knot and the first knot from row 1. Don't pull too hard on the strings or your knot will skew upwards.

Bottle Holder

This macramé bottle holder is stylish, sustainable and practical; a fun and functional project perfect for beginners. Using just a few basic macramé knots, you'll create a hands-free carrier that's ideal for walks, festivals, the gym or everyday errands. It's a great way to stay hydrated on the go while showing off your macramé skills!

SIZE

Approx 80cm (31½in) long, from shoulder to base

MATERIALS

- 42m (46yd) of 5mm braided string

TOOLS

- Measuring tape
- Scissors
- Masking tape
- S hook (optional)
- Beader or crochet hook (optional)

KNOTS USED

- Alternating square knot (page 46)
- Gathering knot (page 36)
- Lark's head knot (page 45)
- Square knot (page 44)

CUT

- 12 x 3.2m (3½yd) of string
- 2 x 70cm (27½in) of string
- 1 x 1.5m (1¾yd) of string

Instructions

1 Take one of the 3.2m (3½yd) strings and create a loop in the middle by crossing over the two strands.

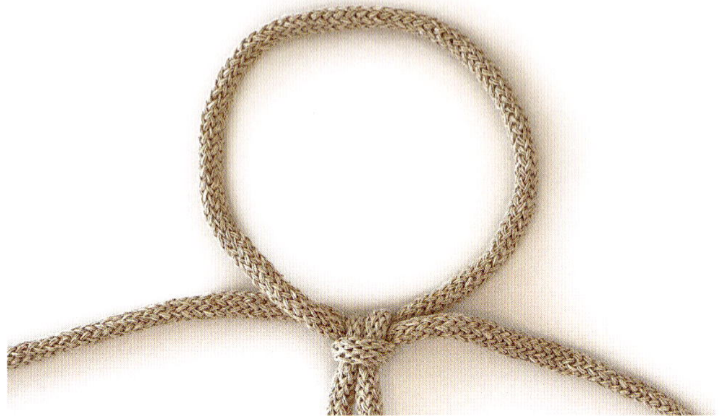

2 Take the next 3.2m (3½yd) string and tie a lark's head knot over the cross by the two strands.

3 Tie all the remaining strings on the loop with the lark's head knot.

4 Pull gently on the two strands that created the cross in step 2, to reduce the size of the loop, until you have created a small circle. Make sure your lark's head knots are tight. The smaller the circle the better.

5 Take one of the strands from step 2, with two strings on the left and one on the right, leave a gap of 4cm (1½in) and tie a square knot.

6 Go around to make five more square knots, so there are six altogether. Keep the gap of 4cm (1½in) consistent.

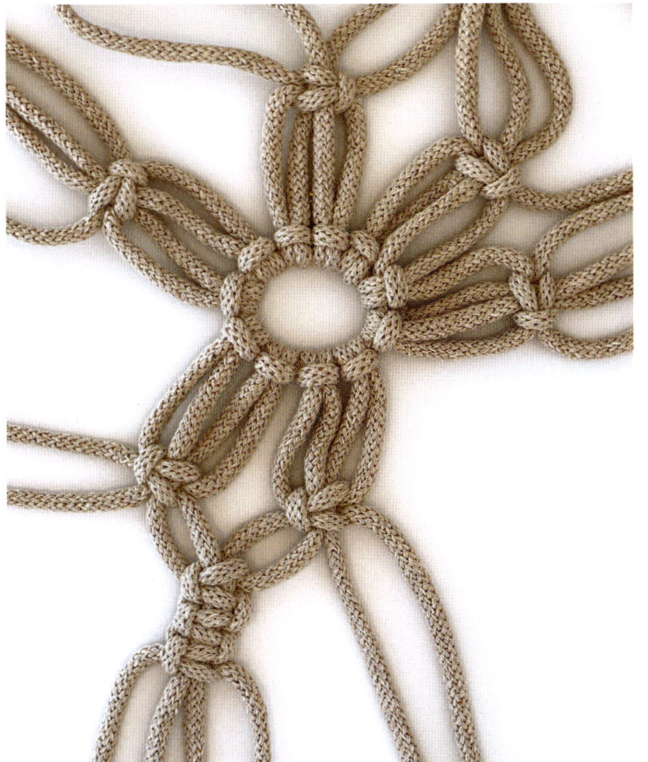

7 Next, leave a gap of 2cm (¾in) and tie an alternating sinnet of three square knots, using two strings from a square knot and two from the square knot next to it, from the previous row.

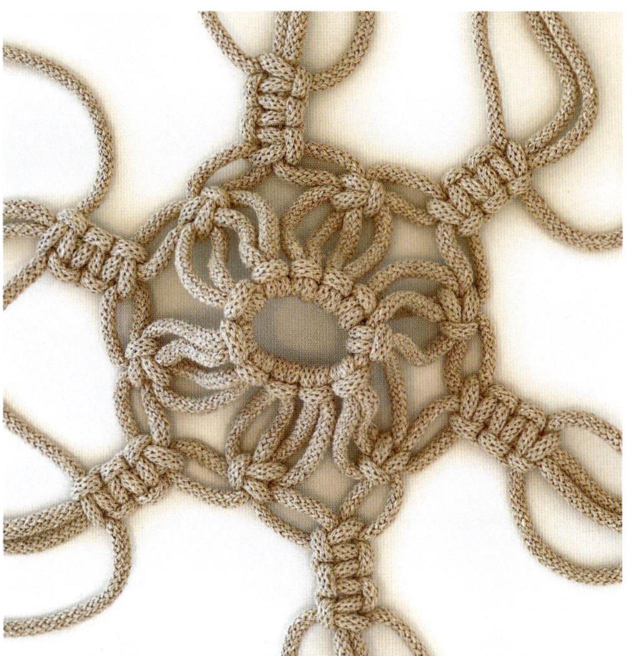

8 Repeat the square knots all around.

9 Leave a gap of 2cm (¾in) and tie an alternating square knot, using two strings from a square knot and two from the square knot next to it, from the previous row.

10 Repeat the square knots all around.

Tip

You can place your water bottle or a spool of string inside the macramé to help you knot, or you can hang the macramé from a S hook.

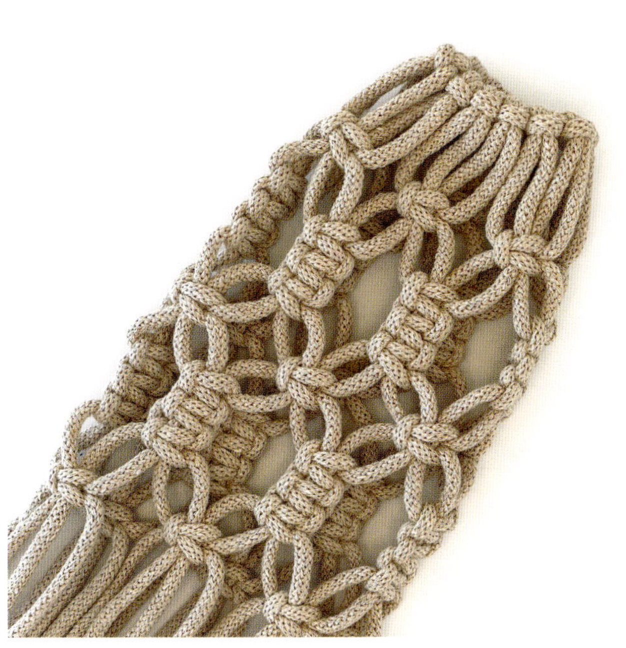

11 Repeat steps 7–10 to form another row of square knots.

12

12 Split the strings into two groups of 12 strings: three square knots on one side and three on the other. Take the first group, leave a gap of 8–10cm (3¼–4in) and tie a gathering knot using the 70cm (27½in) string.

13 Repeat step 12 with the other set of strings, and ensure the two gathering knots are at the same height on either side.

14 Working on the first set of strings, take two strings, the far left and far right, and use them as working strings, to tie sinnets of square knots around the 10 strings in the middle. Tie the square knots tightly and make sure the filler strings are pulled – keep checking the back as you tie the knots. Keep tying square knots until the working strings are 3–5cm (1¼–2in) long.

15 Next, put aside two new long working strings, trim four of the filler strings and keep tying sinnets of square knots with the new working strings around the remaining filler strings and ends of the previous working strings, until you have made a sinnet of square knots, approximately 40cm (15¾in) long.

16 Repeat steps 14 and 15 with the other set.

17 Gather the strings from the two sets together by placing them next to each other, with the ends from each side facing opposite ways. Use a piece of masking tape to hold them together, and check that you are happy with the length of your water bottle holder: you might want to adjust where you overlap the strings and tape them, to increase or decrease the length of the strap.

18 To make the handle, take a 1.5m (1¾yd) piece of string, start from one end and wrap it over all the strings in between the sinnets of square knots. Hold the strings with your right hand and the wrapping strings on the left. Wrap tightly and avoid gaps in between the strings.

19 When you reach the other end, with the help of a beader or crochet hook, tuck in the end of the wrapping string inside the handle.

20 Trim any excess strings to finish.

Techniques

WAVE KNOT

The wave knot is a decorative knot that creates a soft, wave-like pattern in your macramé design – perfect for adding movement and rhythm to wall hangings or to create wearable macramé pieces.

1 Pass the first three strings under the next two strings, as shown.

2 Pass the last string under the three strings, over the two middle strings, into the loop on the left, and under the three strings.

3 Pull gently.

4 Pass the last three strings under the middle two.

5 Pass the first string under the three strings, over the middle two, into the loop on the right, and under the three strings.

6 Pull gently.

Hat Décor

Add a touch of bohemian charm to any hat with this macramé hat décor. This piece is a simple yet eye-catching way to personalize your accessories using just a few basic knots. Whether you're dressing up a wide-brimmed sun hat for the summer or adding flair to your favourite fedora, this project is a quick, creative way to elevate your style with a handmade macramé addition.

SIZE

Approx. 4cm (1½in) deep, 60cm (24in) long, excluding tassel (length can be altered to fit your own hat)

MATERIALS

- 16m (17½yd) of 3mm braided string in natural
- Sun hat of your choice (mine has an internal diameter size of 20cm/7¾in)

TOOLS

- Cork/macramé board and pins
- Measuring tape
- Scissors
- Fabric glue (optional)

KNOTS USED

- Square knot (page 44)
- Wave knot (page 56)

CUT

- 4 x 3.2m (3½yd) of string
- 2 x 1m (1yd) of string
- 1 x 80cm (31½in) of string

A period of grace

Instructions

1 Place from left to right three 3.2m (3½yd) long strings, two 1m (1yd) long strings and one 3.2m (3½yd) long string.

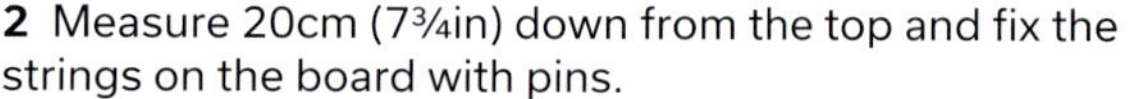

2 Measure 20cm (7¾in) down from the top and fix the strings on the board with pins.

3 Tie a wave knot.

4 Continue making wave knots until you have covered the circumference of your sun hat.

5 If any string is too short, you can use a drop of fabric glue to fix it at the back and trim any excess.

6 Take the 80cm (31½in) length of string and tie three or four square knots around all the strings from the band of wave knots.

7 Trim the string ends to the desired length.

Techniques

DOUBLE HALF HITCH KNOT

This versatile knot creates a linear row of knots and can be worked in a diagonal, straight or vertical line. This is the most common macramé knot after the square knot.

1 Use string 1 as your guide, holding it at an angle or horizontally in front of the other strings. This string is sometimes called the 'holding' or 'static' cord.

2 Use string 2 as your first working string. Pull string 2 up and over string 1, making a loop.

3 Pull gently. You have made a half hitch knot.

4 Repeat steps 1–3, still using string 2.

5 Position the two loops next to each other. The second loop secures the knot. Don't pull too hard when making this knot or you will 'lose' the loops around the guide.

DECREASING ALTERNATING SQUARE KNOTS

This pattern is used to decrease the number of square knots in each row.

1 Tie a row of square knots (see page 44).

2 Start the second row by making a square knot using strings 3 and 4 from the first square knot and strings 1 and 2 from the second square knot. Continue making square knots with the remaining strings, leaving the last two strings untouched. You will have two unused strings on both the left and the right.

3 Start the third row by making a square knot using strings 3 and 4 from the first square knot and strings 1 and 2 from the second square knot of the preview row – you will have four unused strings on the left. Make square knots until you have four remaining strings on both the left and right sides. Continue until the desired pattern is achieved. Usually, until you have a single square knot on your last row.

Clutch Bag

This macramé clutch bag is a chic and unique accessory, a perfect project for those ready to take their skills to the next level. Combining classic knots with a bit of creativity, this stylish bag is both functional and eye-catching. Whether for a night out, a wedding or a casual day, your handmade clutch will add a personal, elegant touch to any outfit.

SIZE

Approx. 20 x 12cm (7¾ x 4¾in)

MATERIALS

- 74m (81yd) of 3mm braided string

TOOLS

- Measuring tape
- Scissors
- Cork or macramé board and pins
- Fabric glue (optional)

KNOTS USED

- Alternating square knot (page 46)
- Decreasing alternating square knot (page 63)
- Double half hitch knot (page 62)
- Square knot (page 44)

CUT

- 24 x 3m (3¼yd) of string
- 2 x 70cm (27½in) of string

Instructions

1 Take two of the 3m (3¼yd) strings, fold them in half and pin them on the board.

2 Tie a square knot.

3 Repeat steps 1–2 with the remaining 22 3m (3½yd) long strings, to make 11 more knots.

4 Pin the 12 square knots on your board next to each other.

5 Tie a row of alternating square knots (see pages 46–47), and make sure all the knots are straight.

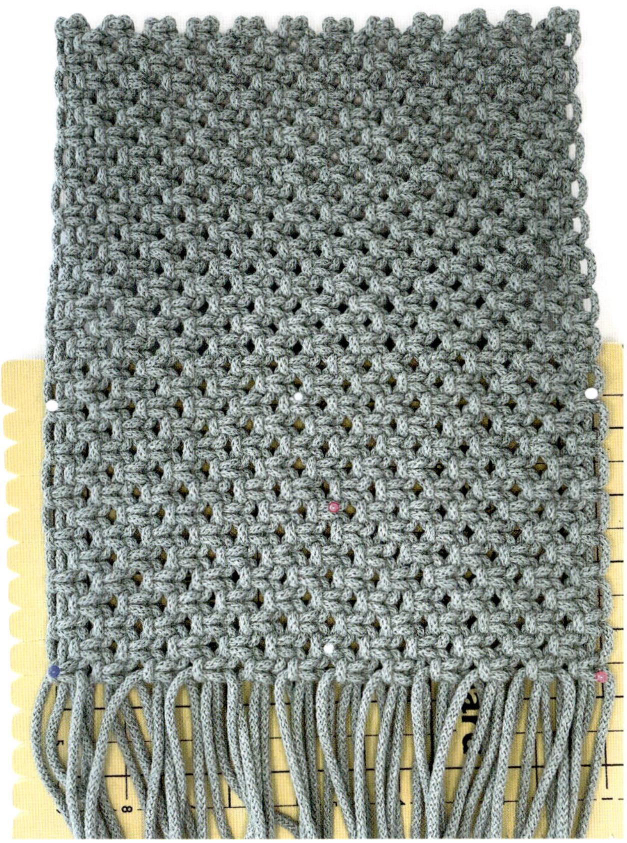

6 Continue tying rows of alternating square knots until you make 33 rows in total.

7 Use the first half of the strings (12 of them), and tie rows of decreasing alternating square knots, by dropping two strings at the start and end of each row, until you have one square knot in the middle.

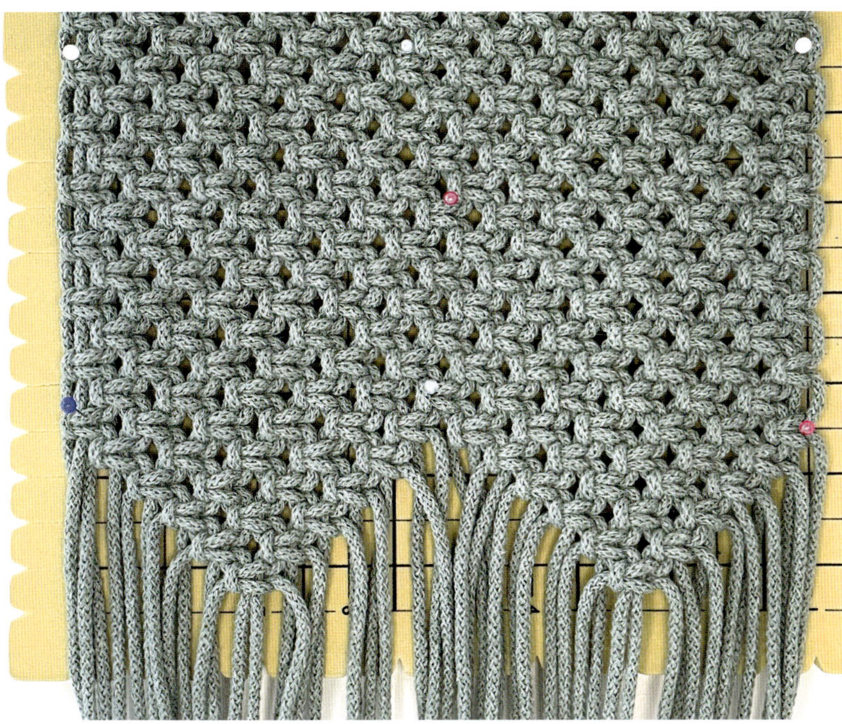

8 Repeat with the remaining 12 strings.

9 Take the middle 16 strings to make a large square knot in between the two triangles of square knots. The middle eight strings are the filler strings and the four strings on the left and right are the working strings.

Tip

Look back to page 29 for how to make a knot with multiple strings.

10 Starting on the left-hand side, take string numbers 3 and 4 from the last square knot and the two strings next on the right, and tie a square knot.

11 Continue tying square knots to make a diagonal line of four square knots until you reach the centre.

12 Repeat on the opposite side.

13 Tie a final square knot with the middle four strings.

14 Next, starting from the left, tie a diagonal line of double half hitch knots under the diagonal line of square knots. Keep the gap between the diagonal lines to a minimum.

15 Repeat on the opposite side and close the two diagonal lines with a double half hitch knot, using the two guide strings.

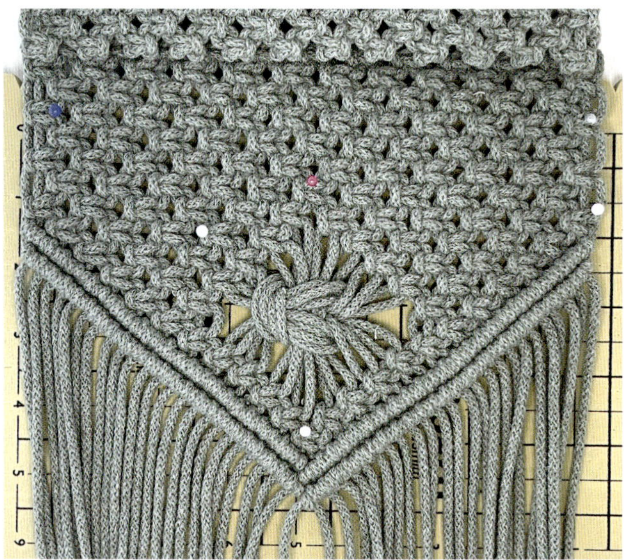

16 Tie a second diagonal line of double half hitch knots underneath on both sides.

17 Next, fold the macramé from the top down. The front part is 15 rows of square knots high: you should have seven loops on each side.

18 Take the 70cm string (27½in), pass it through the top loops and start weaving, zigzagging the string's end through the loops.

19 When you reach the bottom, tie a strong double knot.

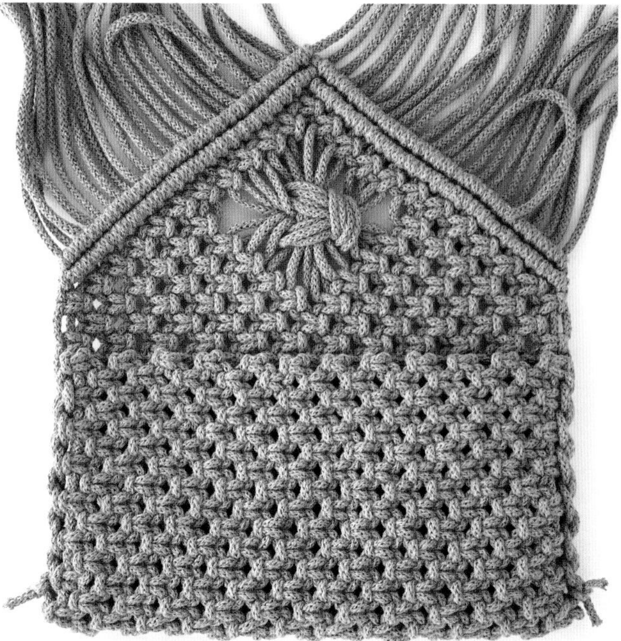

20 Tie another double knot on the other side. This is the inside of the bag.

21 Turn the bag inside out, so that the right sides are facing out.

22 If you would like to keep the fringe, trim the strings at the desired length. See page 26 for more on trimming fringes.

23 Otherwise, trim the strings to 2–3cm (¾–1in) and glue the ends at the back of the double half hitch knots, on the underside of the bag flap. Trim any excess string to finish.

Techniques

VERTICAL LARK'S HEAD KNOT

The vertical lark's head knot is a variation of the classic lark's head, where cords are attached in a vertical orientation instead of horizontal. It's especially useful for creating vertical lines or columns within your design and adding texture to your macramé projects.

1 Take the working string on the right over and under the guide string on the left and through the loop.

2 Take the working string under and over the guide string, through the loop.

3 Pull to tighten the knot.

Tip

Make sure you keep the tension of the knots consistent, especially when tying from one knot to the other.

Vertical lark's head knots are used in the Owl project overleaf.

Owl

Bring a touch of whimsy and style to your space with this modern macramé owl project. Combining traditonal knots and modern techniques with creative flair, this design transforms the classic macramé owl into a charming, contemporary piece. Perfect for adding personality to your home or gifting a loved one, this modern owl blends macramé details with elegant texture.

SIZE

Approx. 40 x 50cm (15¾ x 19¾in)

MATERIALS

- 110m (120yd) of 4mm single-twist string
- Circular metal frame, 25cm (9¾in) diameter
- Two wooden beads, 2cm (¾in) diameter
- Wooden dowel or piece of clean, dry driftwood, approx. 20cm (7¾in) long

TOOLS

- Measuring tape
- Scissors
- Cork or macramé board and pins
- Brush/comb
- Fabric glue/glue gun
- Masking tape

KNOTS USED

- Alternating square knot (page 46)
- Double half hitch knot (page 62)
- Gathering knot (page 36)
- Reversed lark's head knot (page 34)
- Square knot (page 44)
- Vertical lark's head knot (page 74)

CUT

BODY:

- 8 x 4m (4½yd) of string

EARS:

- 12 x 3½m (4yd) of string

WINGS:

- 20 x 20cm (7¾in) of string

Follow the instructions before cutting the strings for the wings

Instructions

EARS

1 Take one 3.5m (4yd) string (this will be your guide string), fold it in half and pin it on the board.

2 Tie on five more strings with reversed lark's head knots.

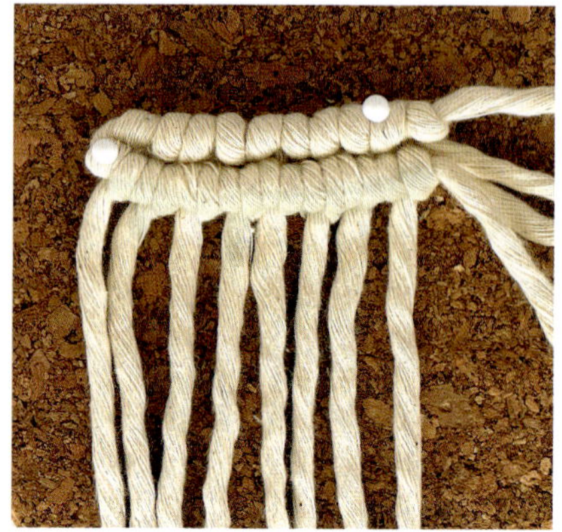

3 Take the end of the guide string at the top, fold it down and tie a line of double half hitch knots using all the strings except the last two.

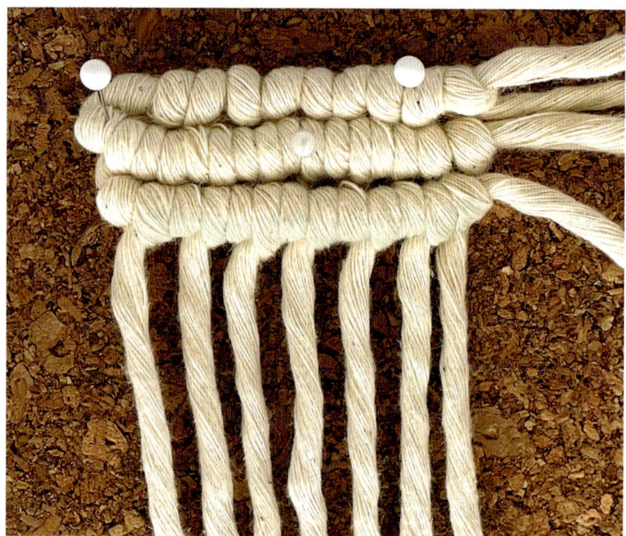

4 Take the string at the top, use it as a guide and tie all the strings from the previous line of double half hitch knots, to make a new line, as shown above.

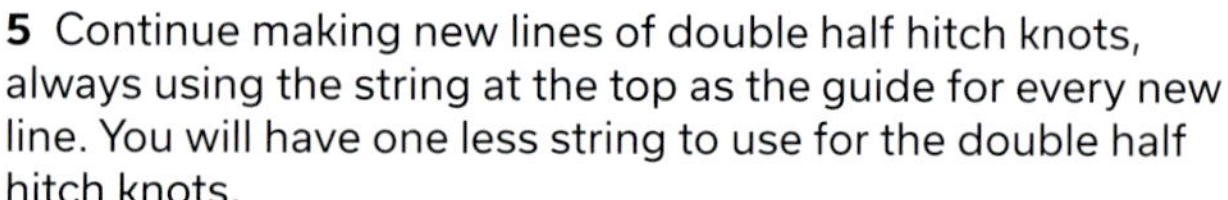

5 Continue making new lines of double half hitch knots, always using the string at the top as the guide for every new line. You will have one less string to use for the double half hitch knots.

6 Continue until you have one last double half hitch knot.

7 Repeat steps 1–6 with the other six strings; make sure you knot the lines of double half hitch knots, from left to right and you will make a mirrored version of the first ear.

Tip

Add a piece of masking tape on the ends of the strings to avoid unravelling.

BODY

8 Tie two 4m (4½yd) strings at the top of the frame with reversed lark's head knots.

9 Tie a square knot.

10 Use reversed lark's head knots to tie two new 4m (4½yd) strings on the frame, one on the left and one on the right of the existing knots. Tie a new row of two alternating square knots.

11 Tie two new 4m (4½yd) strings on the frame, one on the left and one on the right, with reversed lark's head knots, then tie a new row of three alternating square knots.

12 Tie two new strings on the frame, one on the left and one on the right, using reversed lark's head knots and tie a new row of four alternating square knots.

13 Next, drop two strings at the start and end, and tie a row of three alternating square knots. Continue making new rows of decreasing alternating square knots (see page 63) until you have one square knot.

14 Tie the ears to the frame, either side of the square knots as shown, using double half hitch knots.

15 Starting with the ear on the left, count from the top string number 3, use it as a guide and tie strings numbers 2 and 1 onto it to make a diagonal line of double half hitch knots.

16 Continue the diagonal line of double half hitch knots by tying half the strings from the square knots.

17 Take string number 4 from the left ear, use it as a guide and tie a new diagonal line of double half hitch knots.

18 Repeat steps 17–19 with the ear on the right.

19 Tie a square knot with the middle four strings.

20 Counting from the centre outwards, add the wooden beads on strings 7 and 8 on the left and right.

21 Tie a square knot under the beads, using the string either side of the beads.

WINGS

22 Cut 10 pieces of string, each 20cm (7¾in) long, and tie them under the left ear using reversed lark's head knots.

23 Take strings number 1 and 2 and tie a vertical lark's head knot (string number 2 over string number 1) approximately in line with the square knot under the wooden bead.

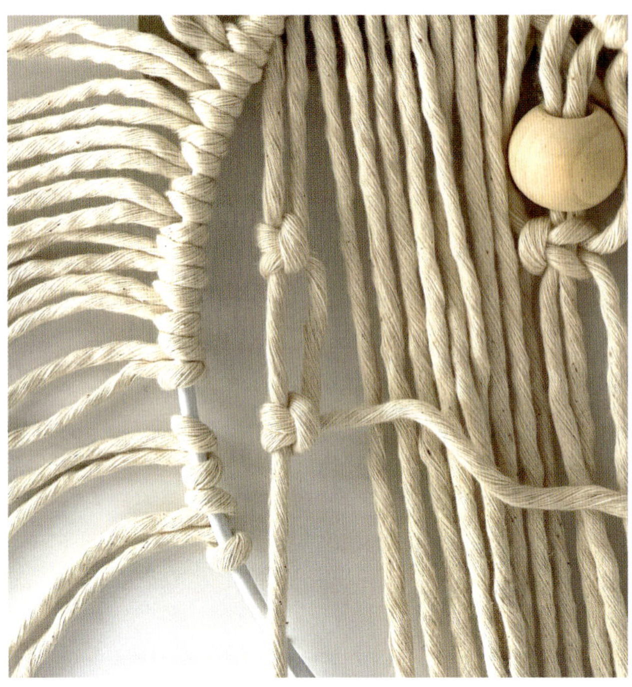

24 Tie a second vertical lark's head knot, leaving a gap of approximately 3cm (1¼in).

25 Slide the second knot up to form a loop.

26 Keep making vertical lark's head knots until you reach the frame below the wing. Fix the two strings on the frame using the double half hitch knots. Keep making steps 23–26 with the other strings.

27 Trim six of the long strings under the wing on the left. Use these leftover strings to cut 10 pieces of string each 20cm (7¾in) long, which you will use for the wing on the right, in the next step.

28 Add the 10 strings (20cm/7¾in) under the right ear using the reversed lark's head knot.

29 Finish making the last vertical lark's head knot sinnet with the remaining two strings and tie the strings on the frame under the wing.

FEET

30 Take the middle eight long strings and split them into two sets. Tie two sinnets of six square knots, leaving a 1cm (½in) gap at the top.

31 Place the wooden dowel on top of the sinnets, fold the sinnets on top of the wooden dowel and pass the strings through the gap at the top. Note: if you have a thinner or thicker dowel than the one I've used, you might need fewer or more knots in your sinnet.

32 Tie a square knot under the wooden dowel to fix each sinnet of square knots.

33 Turn your macramé over and fix any short string at the back with some fabric glue, and once dried trim any excess.

34 Take the remaining long strings, tie a gathering knot under the wooden dowel, using a spare string you cut earlier, a minimum of 60–70cm (23½–27½in) long.

35 Brush the wings and trim to the desired shape. See page 25 for more on brushing fringes.

36 Trim the strings that hang below the gathering knot underneath the dowel to your desired length, and your owl is complete!

BERRY KNOT

Also called a raspberry knot, this is a three-dimensional decorative knot that can be used to add detail and texture. Bear in mind that you will need a lot more length in your strings to make this knot compared to a regular square knot.

1 Make a sinnet of three square knots (see page 44), leaving a gap of about 5mm (¼in) at the top.

2 Take the filler strings up and over the gap in the middle at the top of your first square knot, as shown.

3 Pull the filler strings down, until your sinnet makes a 'bubble'.

4 Secure the knot by making a square knot under your 'bubble'.

Tip

The berry knot uses a lot of string – for each knot you make four square knots. It's good to be aware of this so you don't run out of string mid-way through your own projects when using this knot.

Lampshade

Add a warm, handmade texture to any room with this stylish macramé lampshade project. Perfect for when you feel ready to turn your macramé skills up a notch, this piece combines a variety of knots to create texture for a cozy home décor feel. Challenge your skills and make a unique lampshade that's both functional and a chic statement piece for your home.

SIZE

40cm (15¾in) diameter x 20cm (7¾in) tall

MATERIALS

- 68m (74½yd) of 3mm single-twist string
- White-coated lampshade frame, 40cm (15¾in) diameter
- Small piece of cardboard with a straight edge, for trimming the fringe (optional)

TOOLS

- Measuring tape
- Scissors
- Comb/brush (optional)

KNOTS USED

- Alternating square knots (page 46)
- Berry knot (page 88)
- Double half hitch knot (page 62)
- Lark's head knot (page 45)
- Square knot (page 44)

CUT

- 48 x 1.4m (1½yd) of string
- 2 x 1.5m (1¾yd) of string

SAFETY NOTE

Some bulbs can get a little hot. I recommend using LED bulbs and ensuring that the shade isn't too close to the bulb. You could add a flame-retardant lining or spray to the lampshade

Instructions

1 Tie all the strings on the frame with lark's head knots. You will see 'gaps' between the strings, but that's fine; the spacing will even out as you knot the pattern.

2 Tie a row of square knots. For each square knot use four strands from two lark's head knots.

3 Tie an alternating row of berry knots.

4 Using one of the 1.5m (1¾yd) strings as a guide, tie a line of double half hitch knots under the berry knots.

5 Close the line by tying a double half hitch knot with the guide's ends, in the inside of the shade.

6 Tie three rows of alternating square knots.

7 Use the other 1.5m (1¾yd) strings as a guide and tie a line of double half hitch knots underneath the square knots. Repeat step 5 to close.

8 Tie a row of square knots. Ensure the knots mirror the line of square knots above the line of double half hitch knots.

9 Pull the knots tight and trim the fringe. You can use a template to help you trim a consistent fringe – cut a piece of cardboard to the desired length and use it as a guide to trim against.

Tip

There are multiple options for the fringe: brush the fringe if you want a fluffy look and then trim it again; leave the fringe as it is; or brush just the end of the fringe, like mine in the photo on page 91.

Techniques

WATERFALL KNOT

The waterfall knot is a beautiful decorative knot, often used to create a cascading, layered effect or in patterns to create flowers. It's perfect for adding texture to wall hangings, plant hangers or statement pieces.

1 Pass a new string inside the lark's head knot (or reversed lark's head knot) with equal ends on each side.

2 Tighten the lark's head knot (or reversed lark's head knot).

3 Working with the new string, place the strand on the left over the right, making a cross on top of the middle two strings.

4 Working with the middle two strings, take the strand on the left and pass it through the loop on the left. Next, take the strand on the right and pass it through the loop on the right.

5 Gently pull the strings, alternating between pulling the new string and the middle two strings.

6 Continue until you have tightened the knot.

Daisy Mini Wreath

Celebrate the beauty of nature with this charming macramé daisy mini wreath. This delicate project combines simple knots to create a timeless floral wreath. Whether hung on a door or wall, or used as a table centrepiece, the daisy mini wreath adds a touch of handmade sunshine to your home.

SIZE

15cm (6in) diameter, excluding bow

MATERIALS

- 5mm braided string in three colours of your choice. Refer to 'Cut' section below for quantities.
- 30cm (12in) of 1mm string in natural colour for hanging the wreath

TOOLS

- Cork/macramé board and pin
- Measuring tape
- Scissors
- Beader or crochet hook

KNOTS USED

- Reversed lark's head knot (page 34)
- Square knot (page 44)
- Vertical lark's head knot (page 74)
- Waterfall knot (page 96)

CUT

- 1 x 2.5m (2¾yd) of white string
- 1 x 2.5m (2¾yd) of olive string
- 1 x 1.2m (1½yd) of yellow string
- 1 x 80cm (31½in) of yellow string
- 1 x 30cm (12in) of 1mm string

Instructions

1 Pin the 1.2m (1½yd) yellow string on the board.

2 Take the white string and tie a reversed lark's head knot in the middle of the olive string. Place it over the yellow string and hold it in place with a pin.

3 Take the white strand on the right and tie the first half of the vertical lark's head knot.

4 Take the yellow string and place it over the number 2 white string going from the right to the left.

5 Finish tying the vertical lark's head knot.

6 Take the white strand on the left, tie the first half of the vertical lark's head knot.

7 Take the yellow string and place it over the number 1 white string.

8 Finish tying the vertical lark's head knot.

9 Fold the olive strings at the top of the other strings, going the opposite way to make a loop.

10 Tie a waterfall knot to complete the daisy. You can pull the yellow string a little, with the help of a crochet hook, to make the centre pop-out.

11 Tie a square knot using the olive strings.

12 Tie a waterfall knot with the white strings.

13 Repeat steps 3–12 to make a chain of 12 daisies.

14 Pass the olive strings through the reversed lark's head knot to close the wreath, with the ends facing opposite ways.

15 Pull the olive strings.

16 If any strings are too short, you can tuck them at the back of the knots.

17 Gather all the strings and, using the 80cm (30½in) string, tie a bow around them.

18 Trim the strings to the desired length.

19 If you wish to hang your wreath, take a piece of thin string, approximately 30cm (12in) long, tie a reversed lark's head knot on the back of the middle square knot at the top of the wreath, and tie a simple knot to form a hanging loop.

ALTERNATING HALF HITCH KNOT

This is a great knot for when you want to use just two strings to create a cord. With this knot, you need to keep alternating the working string and the filler string. I have used different colours here for clarity.

1 Start by tying a half hitch knot (see steps 1–3 on page 62).

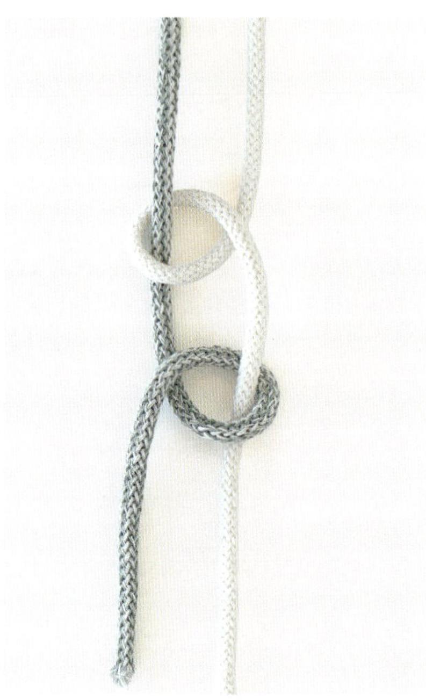

2 Alternate your working string and filler string to tie a new half hitch.

3 Repeat steps 1 and 2 until the desired length is reached.

Tip

The half hitch knot is half of the double half hitch knot you learnt on page 62 – steps 1–3 of the double half hitch create the half hitch knot.

Alternating half hitch knots are used in the Wall Hanging project overleaf.

Wall Hanging

Capture the free-spirited essence of bohemian style with this beautiful macramé wall hanging. Combining a mix of classic knots and flowing textures, this project lets you express creativity while adding an arty vibe to any room. Perfect for beginners ready to make a timeless statement piece, this is a stylish addition to your home décor.

SIZE

50 x 70cm (19¾ x 27½in)

MATERIALS

- 50m (54¾yd) of 5mm braided string in natural
- 45m (49yd) of 5mm braided string in mustard
- Wooden dowel, 50cm (19¾in) long

TOOLS

- Measuring tape
- Scissors
- Two S hooks or masking tape

KNOTS USED

- Alternating half hitch knot (page 106)
- Alternating square knot (page 46)
- Double half hitch knot (page 62)
- Lark's head knot (page 45)
- Square knot (page 44)
- Vertical lark's head knot (page 74)

CUT

PART 1

- 1 x 2.5m (2¾yd) of string in natural
- 2 x 1.8m (2yd) of string in mustard
- 2 x 1.8m (2yd) of string in natural
- 2 x 1.4m (1½yd) of string in mustard
- 2 x 1.4m (1½yd) of string in natural

PART 2

- 2 x 2.2m (2½yd) of string in mustard
- 2 x 2.2m (2½yd) of string in natural

PART 3

- 6 x 3.8m (4¼yd) of string in mustard
- 4 x 3.8m (4¼yd) of string in natural

PART 4 (fringes)

Refer to the steps on page 119 for quantities and length

Instructions

For larger projects such as this, it's easier to work in parts. This project has four parts.

PART 1

1 Take the 2.5m (2¾yd) long natural string and tie it in the middle of the dowel with a lark's head knot – this will be the lead string.

Tips

I recommend you hang your macramé on the S hooks on a clothes rail, door or on the back of a chair. Alternatively, you can use masking tape to fix the dowel to a flat surface.

Remember to take breaks and do gentle stretches in between knotting.

2 Tie the 1.8m (2yd) long mustard strings with lark's head knots, one on the end of the lead string on the left, and one on the right.

3 Tie a square knot with the mustard strings.

4 Tie the 1.8m (2yd) long natural strings with the lark's head knot, one on the end of the lead string on the left, and one on the right.

5 Tie a row of two alternating square knots, under the first square knot.

6 Tie the 1.4m (1½yd) long mustard strings with the lark's head knot, one on the end of the lead string on the left, and one on the right.

7 Tie a row of three alternating square knots.

8 Tie the 1.4m (1½yd) long natural strings with the lark's head knot, one on the end of the lead string on the left, and one on the right.

9 Tie a row of four alternating square knots.

10 Next, tie a row of three alternating square knots, followed by a row of two alternating square knots and a final square knot with the middle four strings.

11 Take the end of the lead string on the left and tie a vertical lark's head knot on the dowel with a gap of 8cm (3¼in) from the lark's head knot in the middle.

12 Repeat with the end of the lead string on the right.

PART 2

1 Tie the 2.2m (2½yd) mustard string next to the vertical lark's head knot, with a lark's head knot, and then the 2.2m (2½yd) string in natural.

2 Use the white and mustard strings to tie a sinnet of alternating half hitches long enough to sit below part 1 of the wall hanging.

3 Repeat steps 1 and 2 on the opposite side.

4 Tie a square knot using the white strings as working strings and the mustard strings as filler strings.

PART 3

1 Tie five of the 3.8m (4¼yd) strings on the dowel, with the lark's head knot, next to part 2, alternating the colours, starting with the mustard first.

2 Take string number 6, use it as a guide and tie a diagonal line of double half hitch knots, going from the centre to the right.

3 Take string number 5, use it as a guide and tie a diagonal line of double half hitch knots, going from the centre to the left.

5

4 Tie a square knot with the middle eight strings. Use the mustard strings as the working strings and the white strings as filler strings.

5 Close the diamond by tying two diagonal lines of double half hitch knots. Join the two diagonal lines by tying a double half hitch with the two guides.

6 Keep making diamonds following steps 1–5 until you have made six of them or a band long enough to reach the middle of the wall hanging.

Tip

To make it easier to check that the sizes are consistent on both bands, you can alternate making the diamonds from the band to the left and to the right.

8

7 Repeat steps 1–6 on the opposite side of the wall hanging.

8 Work on the left band to complete the diagonal line of double half hitch knots, going from left to right.

9 Repeat on the opposite side.

10 Close the bands with a double half-hitch knot using the guides.

11 Use the middle 12 strings and tie two diagonal lines of double half hitch knots to create the top of a new diamond shape.

12 Tie a square knot using the eight middle strings. Use the white strings as working strings and the mustard strings as filler strings.

13 Close the diamond by tying two diagonal lines of double half hitch knots. Join the two diagonal lines by tying a double half hitch knot with the two guides.

PART 4 – FRINGES

Note: please read through the steps below before cutting the strings for your fringes as you might want to add more or fewer strings and have longer or shorter fringes than mine.

For the part 1 fringes I used:
Eight 90cm (35½in) strings in mustard; six 90cm (35½in) strings in natural.

For the part 3 fringes I used:
Twenty-two 70cm (27½in) strings in natural; five 70cm (27½in) strings in mustard.

1 Tie the strings on the lead string, with a lark's head knot, alternating the colours. Place five strings on each side.

2 Starting from the top of the band, tie a white string with a lark's head knot on the outer string.

3 Next, on the outer strings in between the diamond, tie a white, mustard and a white string.

4 Repeat step 2 with all the gaps between the diamonds.

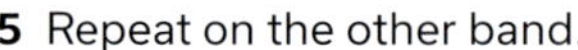

5 Repeat on the other band.

6 Take the lead's ends and tie a simple knot to create a loop to use to hang the wall hanging.

7 Trim the fringes and strings to the desired length.

Moving on

You've got the basics – great work! And here's the exciting part: this is only the start of your macramé journey. Once you get comfortable with the basic knots, there's a whole world of cool, more complex patterns and projects waiting for you. More knots, new patterns, bigger and more challenging projects, but all within reach, now that you have mastered the foundations of macramé. So, get excited, keep experimenting and watch your skills (and creations!) grow in amazing ways. In this section are a few ideas that you can start experimenting with next.

ADDING COLOUR

You can add colour by tying a different coloured string on two strands and tying square knots, for example.

You could also tie half square knots and alternate the working strings to create sinnets of half square knots in different colours.

This is a great technique to use for making plant hangers and wall hangings.

1 Adding a second colour using the square knot (see page 44).

2 Adding a second colour using the half square knot (see page 35).

SQUARE KNOT SINNET

The square knot sinnet is a versatile and classic macramé technique that creates a sturdy, textured braid perfect for a variety of projects. By repeating square knots in a vertical row, you can craft everything from plant hangers to coasters and heart shapes. The trick is to keep the tension of the knots consistent. I recommend tying the sinnet of square knots in one go if you can.

1 Take two 80cm (31½in) strings and pin them on a board.

2 Take one 8m (8¾yd) string and tie a sinnet of square knots until you have run out of string. Trim the excess strings.

3 You could roll up and glue the sinnet of square knots to create a round coaster (above). Alternatively, roll the sinnet into a heart shape, glue the ends and add a hanging loop to make a sweet decoration (below).

3D MACRAMÉ

Another reason I love macramé is its versatility, and how we can use the same pattern to make something simple into something more complex looking.

You can play with colours and sizes to create a beautiful 3D macramé piece, or add the 3D pieces to a wall hanging for extra detail and texture.

MACRAMÉ LEAF NECKLACE

To make a single leaf, I used 6m (6½yd) of 1.5mm cotton string, and cut this into the following lengths:

- 7 x 80cm (32in)
- 1 x 30cm (12in)

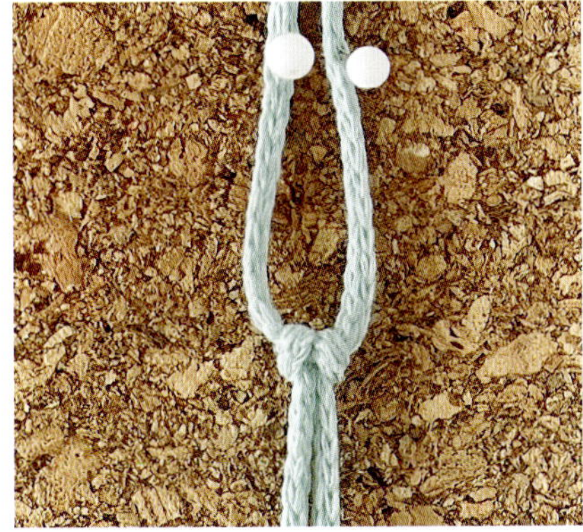

1 Take one of the 80cm (31½in) strings, fold it in half and fix it onto the board. Take another 80cm (31½in) string and fix it onto the first one with a reversed lark's head knot.

2 Take another 80cm (31½in) string, place the middle under the string on the left coming from the reversed lark's head knot, and tie a double half hitch knot. With the same string, tie a new double half-hitch knot on the string on the right coming from the reversed lark's head knot. Slide the knots to the top. Add all the remaining 80cm (31½in) of string following steps 3 and 4.

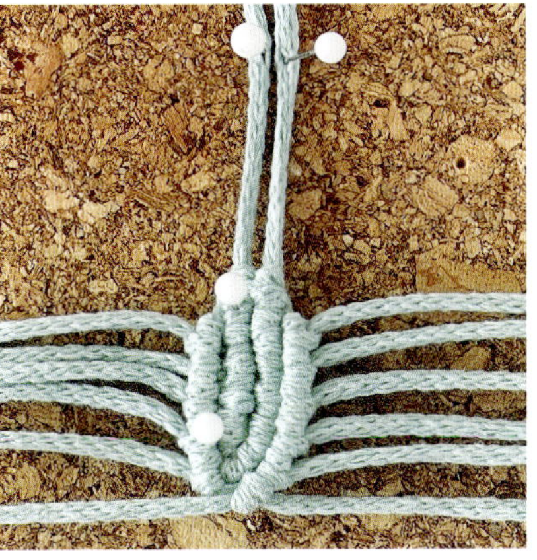

3 Tie a double half hitch knot with the middle two strings. You now have six strings on each side. Take the top string on the left; this is your guide string. Place it over all the strings on the left and tie a line of double half hitch knots, going from top to bottom. Repeat on the other side.

4 Continue tying lines of double half hitch knots on both sides, until you have made a total of seven. To close the leaf shape, start a new line of double half hitch knots on the left, by making the first double half hitch knot with the first string.

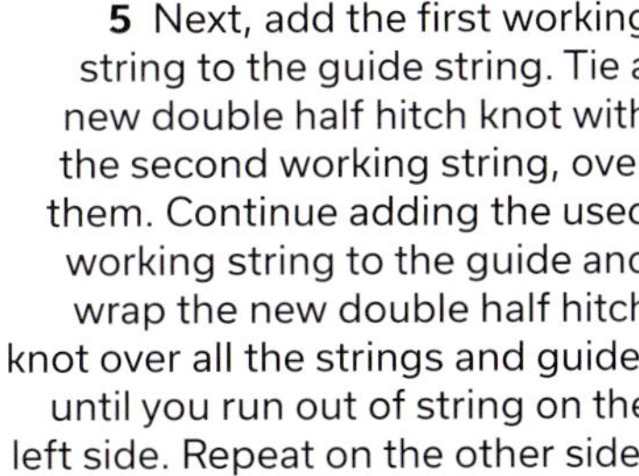

5 Next, add the first working string to the guide string. Tie a new double half hitch knot with the second working string, over them. Continue adding the used working string to the guide and wrap the new double half hitch knot over all the strings and guide, until you run out of string on the left side. Repeat on the other side.

Continued overleaf...

6 Turn the leaf and tie a gathering knot with the 30cm (12in) string.

7 Trim the fringe to the desired length and tie a simple knot to close the string for the necklace.

A simple leaf shape could make a bag charm or necklace – make a few of them all the same, gather them together and it becomes a beautiful macramé flower!

LACE DETAIL

Add a delicate, airy touch to your macramé wall hangings by incorporating lace-like details. Perfect for elevating simple pieces into something truly special, lace details add texture and charm with a simple knot. Use the vertical double half hitch knots you learned in the Owl project on page 76 to create a lace detail in your macramé, instead of having the classic straight lines of double half hitch knots. This simple detail can add character to your macramé, as shown above.

DIAMONDS OF HALF HITCH KNOTS

To create a beautiful diamond pattern, you can tie double diagonal lines of double half hitch knots, tie square knots with the guide lines, which can be in a different colour, and then continue your double diagonal lines of double half hitch knots. You can add extra details by weaving the strings in between the diamonds. This pattern is perfect to create larger home décor such as rugs, cushions, wall hangings and table runners.

SCALING

Something else I love about macramé is that the same project made with a different type of string, for example thicker or finer, gives a different look and feel. I often experiment with scaling for jewellery and accessories like keychains and belts.

Index